August, 2004

My Dear Peggy,

What a privilege it
has been to watch you--
my daughter & firstborn --
mother your daughter &
first born. Your love &
patience are the greatest
gifts you will ever give
to dear Amelia. You are
"off" to a splendid motherhood.

Love & support always,
XO Mom XO

To a very special
Mother ...

To a very special
Mother ...

This is a Parragon Publishing Book
This edition published in 2003

Parragon Publishing
Queen Street House
4 Queen Street
Bath BA1 1HE, UK

This book was created by Magpie Books,
an imprint of Constable & Robinson Ltd.

Designed by Tony and Penny Mills

A copy of the British Library Cataloguing-in-Publication Data
is available from the British Library

Printed in Italy

ISBN 1-84273-525-X

INTRODUCTION

other's love, so freely given over the years, remains like an inner fire within her child throughout the whole of life, warming, comforting and consoling. This book brings together a collection of tributes and reflections upon motherhood. The mother who was awake in the middle of the night feeding her baby is again awake twenty years later, waiting to hear the tread upon the stair to tell her her child is safely home again. Through all these years she has fed and clothed and inspired her child; they have celebrated holidays and birthdays in love and happiness. No book would be long or full enough to say thank you.

Mothers hold their
children's hands for a little
while and their hearts
forever.

IRISH SAYING

7

Mother is the person who, seeing there are only two pieces of pie for three people, at once claims that she never did care for pie.

ANON

When I was a child I had to sit with all the grown ups and eat exactly what they were having; I had to sit there until we all got down and I was never allowed to speak unless spoken to. I have let my children eat what and when they like—and all they like is beefburgers and beans and ice cream. I wonder who was right.

EILEEN JARVIS

THE LOVE OF A MOTHER

A father may turn his back on his child; brothers and sisters may become inveterate enemies; husbands may desert their wives and wives their husbands. But a mother's love endures through all; in good repute, in bad repute, in the face of the world's condemnation, a mother still loves on, and still hopes that her child may turn from his evil ways, and repent; still she remembers the infant smiles that once filled her bosom with rapture, the merry laugh, the joyful shout of his childhood, the opening promise of his youth; and she can never be brought to think him all unworthy.

WASHINGTON IRVING

(1783—1859)

Of all the rights of women, the greatest
is to be a Mother.

LIN YUTANG

The heart of a Mother is a deep abyss at the
bottom of which you will always find
forgiveness.

HONORÉ DE BALZAC (1799—1850)

There never was a child so lovely but his
mother was glad to get him asleep.

RALPH WALDO EMERSON (1803—1882)

A LESSON FOR

MAMA

Dear Mother, if you just could be
A tiny little girl like me,
And I your mother, you would see
    How nice I'd be to you.
I'd always let you have your way;
I'd never frown at you and say,
    "You're behaving ill to-day;
    Such conduct will not do."

I'd always give you jelly-cake
For breakfast and I'd never shake
My head and say, "You must not take
     So very large a slice."
I'd never say, "My dear I trust
You will not make me say you *must*
Eat up your oatmeal"; or "The crust
     You'll find is very nice."

     I'd buy you candy every day;
I'd go down town with you and say,
"What would my darling like? You may
     Have anything you see."
I'd never say, "My pet you know,
'Tis bad for health and teeth, and so
I cannot let you have it. No;
     It would be wrong of me."

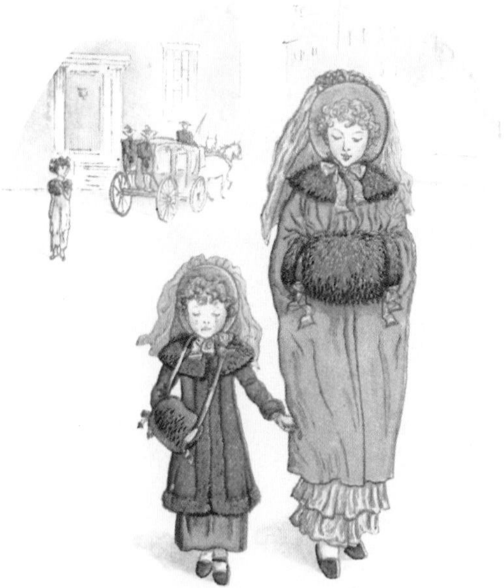

I'd never say. "Well, just a *few!*"
I'd let you stop your lessons too;
I'd say, "They are too hard for you,
  Poor child, to understand."
    I'd put the books and slates away;
You shouldn't do a thing but play,
And have a party every day;
    Ah-h-h! wouldn't that be grand!

But, mother dear, you cannot grow
Into a little girl, you know,
And I can't be your mother; so
    The only thing to do
Is just for you to try and see
How very, very nice 'twould be
For you to do all this for me,
Now, mother couldn't you?

SYDNEY DAYRE

18

My mother was the making of me.
THOMAS EDISON

Who takes the child by the hand takes the
mother's heart.
GERMAN PROVERB

Your mother is always your mother, even when
she is your best friend and champion.
JAN DONOVAN

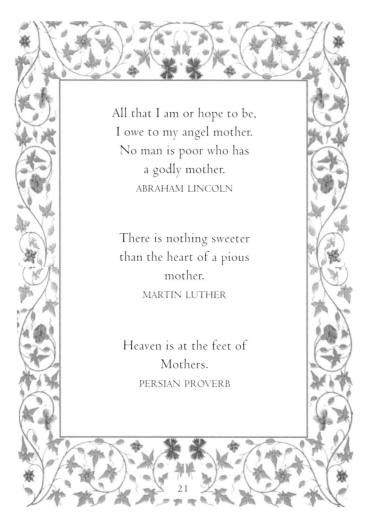

All that I am or hope to be,
I owe to my angel mother.
No man is poor who has
a godly mother.
ABRAHAM LINCOLN

There is nothing sweeter
than the heart of a pious
mother.
MARTIN LUTHER

Heaven is at the feet of
Mothers.
PERSIAN PROVERB

The greatest love is a mother's;
then comes a dog's;
then comes a sweetheart's.

POLISH PROVERB

They always looked back before turning the corner, for their mother was always at the window to nod and smile, and wave her hand at them. Somehow it seemed as if they couldn't have got through the day without that, for whatever their mood might be, the last glimpse of that motherly face was sure to affect them like sunshine.

LOUISA MAY ALCOTT (1832—1888)
from *Little Women*

A Mother is not a person to lean on but a
person who has made leaning unnecessary.

ANON

Never marry a man who dislikes his mother.
He will end up disliking you.

AGONY AUNT

A suburban mother's role is to deliver children
obstetrically once, and by car forever after.

PETER DE VRIES

The hand that rocks the cradle
Is the hand that rules the world.

W. R. WALLACE

Let France have good Mothers, and she will
have good sons.

NAPOLEON I

All mothers are working mothers.

ANON

An ounce of Mother is worth a ton of priest.

SPANISH PROVERB

SONG

Oh, baby, baby, baby dear,
We lie alone together here;
The snowy gown and cap and sheet
With lavender are fresh and sweet;
Through half-closed blinds the roses
    peer
To see and love you, baby dear.

We are so tired, we like to lie
Just doing nothing, you and I
within the darkened quiet room.
The sun sends dusk rays through the
    gloom,
Which is no gloom since you are here,
My little life, my baby dear.

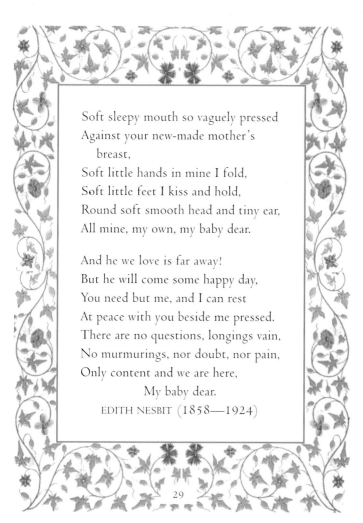

Soft sleepy mouth so vaguely pressed
Against your new-made mother's
    breast,
Soft little hands in mine I fold,
Soft little feet I kiss and hold,
Round soft smooth head and tiny ear,
All mine, my own, my baby dear.

And he we love is far away!
But he will come some happy day,
You need but me, and I can rest
At peace with you beside me pressed.
There are no questions, longings vain,
No murmurings, nor doubt, nor pain,
Only content and we are here,
        My baby dear.

EDITH NESBIT (1858—1924)

29

Mother's love is peace. It need not be acquired,
it need not be deserved.

ERICH FROMM

The world has no such flowers in any land,
And no such pearl in any gulf the sea
As any babe on any mother's knee.

ALGERNON CHARLES SWINBURNE
Pelagius

The future destiny of the child is always the
work of the Mother.

NAPOLEON BONAPARTE

Perhaps when time shall add a few
Short months to thee, thou'lt love me too;
And after that, through life's long way
Become my sure and cheering stay:
Wilt care for me and be my hold,
When I am weak and old.

Thou'lt listen to my lengthen'd tale,
And pity me when I am frail—
—But see! the sweepy swimming fly
Upon the window takes thine eye.
Go to thy little senseless play;
Thou doest not heed my lay.

JOANNA BAILLIE
(1762—1851)
from
A Mother to her Waking Infant

A mother is the only person on earth who can
divide her love among all her children and each
child still have all her love.

ANON

Children are the anchors that
hold a mother to life.

SOPHOCLES

Mother is the name for God in the lips and
hearts of little children.

WILLIAM M. THACKERAY

The Mother's
heart is the child's
schoolroom.
HENRY WARD
BEECHER
(1813—1887)

Who ran to help me when I fell,
And would some pretty story tell,
Or kiss the place to make it well?
My Mother

ANN TAYLOR
(1782—1866)

My Mum is a mechanic,
She fixes people's cars,
She hits them and she hammers them
With gigantic iron bars.

My Mum is my mechanic,
I'm her favourite machine,
She feeds me and she washes me
Till I am squeaky clean.

T. S. PROUST (AGE 11)

My Mother was the most beautiful woman I
ever saw. All I am I owe to my Mother. I
attribute all my success in life to the moral,
intellectual and physical education I received
from her.
GEORGE WASHINGTON (1732—1799)

Whatsoever I shall be able to do I acknowledge
to be a debt to you from whom I had that
education which must make my fortune ...
JOHN DONNE,
poet, to his mother (c. 1616)

Late home
No time to phone and
Creeping up the stairs
A light clicks off
A small cough
A sigh and then another
Who is it who cares?
Whose sleepless nightmares?
Who? It's Mother

YOLANDE YOUNG

She told me not to dye my hair,
She said I'd look a sight,
I dyed it blue; I didn't care,
But Oh, dear, she was right.

WENDY HOPE

Youth fades; love droops,
the leaves of friendship fall;
A Mother's secret hope outlives them all.
OLIVER WENDELL HOLMES (1809—1894)

All women become like their mothers. That is
their tragedy. No man does. That's his.
OSCAR WILDE
The Importance of Being Earnest (1895)

Oliver, you must be clean
I tell you every day
But Mother, that is very mean
I like myself this way.

Why can't I, if and when I please,
Be conspicuously dirty
Oh, Oliver, you shouldn't tease,
You know you're one and thirty.
JOHN KATES (1822—1911)

To a mother, a son is never a
fully grown man; and a son
is never a fully grown man
until he understands and
accepts this about his mother.

ANON

A man loves his sweetheart the most, his wife
the best, but his mother the longest.
IRISH PROVERB

Men are what their mothers made them.
RALPH WALDO EMERSON

A man who has been the indisputable favorite
of his mother keeps for life the feeling of a
conqueror, that confidence of success that
often induces real success.
SIGMUND FREUD

MOTHER

Sylvia hastened home, feeling as if she had been absent long; her mother stood on the little knoll at the side of the house watching for her, with her hand shading her eyes from the low rays of the setting sun: but as soon as she saw her daughter in the distance, she returned to her work, whatever that might be. She was not a woman of many words, or of much demonstration; few observers would have guessed how much she loved her child; but Sylvia, without any reasoning or observation, instinctively knew that her mother's heart was bound up in her.

ELIZABETH GASKELL
Sylvia's Lovers

Making the decision to have a child—it's
momentous. It is to decide forever to have
your heart go walking around outside
your body.

ANON

Life began with waking up and loving my
mother's face.

GEORGE ELIOT

It is at our mother's knee
that we acquire our noblest
and truest and highest
ideals.

MARK TWAIN

No matter how old a mother is, she
watches her middle-aged children for
signs of improvement.

FLORINDA SCOTT-MAXWELL

Oh what a power is
motherhood, possessing
A potent spell
All women alike
Fight fiercely for a child.

EURIPIDES

MOTHER

She is my first, great love. She was a wonder-
ful, rare woman—you do not know; as strong,
and steadfast, and generous as the sun. She
could be as swift as a white whiplash, and as
kind and gentle as warm rain, and as steadfast
as the irreducible earth beneath us.

D. H. LAWRENCE

I remember my Mother's prayers and they have
always followed me.
They have clung to me all my life.

ABRAHAM LINCOLN

(1809—1865)

A man's work is from sun to sun, but a mother's
work is never done.

ANON

Girls migrate from the age of four—the first
time they disown you at the school gate—and
only truly return when they become mothers
themselves.

JOYCE WILBY

God could not be everywhere and
therefore He made mothers.

JEWISH PROVERB

…Yet love thy dead, who long lay in thine arms:
And when thy loss shall be repaid with gains
Look to my little babes, my dear remains.
And if thou love thyself, or loved'st me
These O protect from stepdame's injury.

ANNE BRADSTREET (C 1613—1672)

Letter to her Husband
before the Birth of one of her Children
(she did not expect to survive)

We've had to make sacrifices. We never used to go abroad for our holidays and we could never afford a new car; but now, at Christmas, and on my birthday, with my three children and five grandchildren sitting round the dining room table, I don't think anyone could have enjoyed a happier and a richer life.

GRACE MORTON

What art's for a woman? To hold on her knees
  Both darlings! To feel all their arms around her
    throat,
Cling, strangle a little! To sew by degrees
  And 'broider the long-clothes and neat little coat
    To dream and to dote.
            ELIZABETH BARRETT BROWNING
              from *Mother and Poet*
            (*Turin after News from Gatea, 1861*)

The children, alone with their mother, told her all about the day's happenings, everything. Nothing had really taken place in them until it was told to their mother.

                D. H. LAWRENCE
                (1885—1930)
                from *Sons and Lovers*

Can a mother sit and hear
An infant groan an infant fear
No, No! never can it be!
Never, never can it be!

WILLIAM BLAKE
"On Another's Sorrow" from
Songs of Innocence (1789)

Happy he
With such a mother!
Faith in womankind
Beats with his blood.

ALFRED, LORD TENNYSON

There never was a woman like her. She was
gentle as a dove and brave as a lioness ... The
memory of my mother and her teachings were,
after all, the only capital I had to start life
with, and on that capital I have made my way.

ANDREW JACKSON

As is the mother
So is her daughter.

EZEKIEL, CHAPTER 16

A lily lasts a day
A rose a week
But a mother's love stays
with us always.

TAMZIN TELFORD

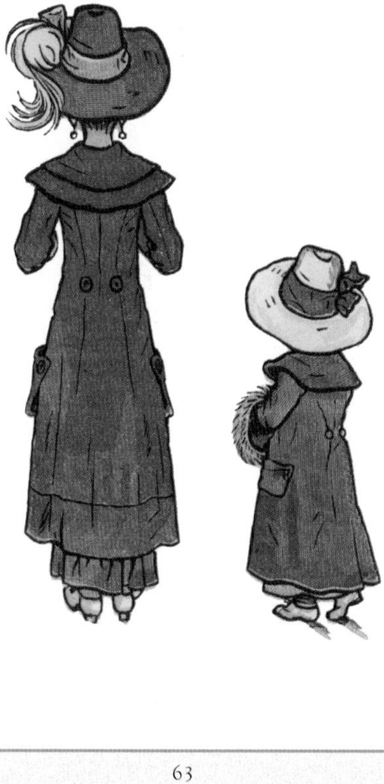

Acknowledgements

Jacket picture Morning, 1910 (oil on canvas) by Boris Mihajlovic Kustodiev (1878–1927). State Russian Museum, St. Petersburg, Russia/Bridgeman Art Library.

page 9 The Grace c.1741–1742 by Jean-Baptiste Simeon Chardin (1699–1779). Louvre, Paris, France/Bridgeman Art Library.

page 13 Out of reach, daughters of Eve, 1895 (w/c) by Sir Frank Dicksee (1853–1928). Chris Beetles Ltd., London, UK/Bridgeman Art Library.

page 18 Musing on the Future, by George Smith (1829–1901). Mallett & Son Antiques Ltd., London, UK/Bridgeman Art Library.

page 24 Mother and Child, 1903 by Carl Larsson (1853–1919). Thiel Gallery, Stockholm, Sweden/Bridgeman Art Library.

page 30 Miss Lily's Return from the Ball by James Hayllar (1829–1920). Mallett & Son Antiques Ltd., London, UK/Bridgeman Art Library.

page 35 Dutch Interior with Mother and Children (oil on canvas) by Bernard Jean Corneille Pothast (1882–1966). We have been unable to trace the copyright holder of this painting and would be grateful to receive any information as to their identity.

page 38 The Music Lesson (La leçon de musique) by Louis Aubert (fl.1740–80). Musée de Picardie, Amiens, France/Giraudon/Bridgeman Art Library.

page 42 The Artist and her Mother (oil on panel) by Rolinda Sharples (1794–1838). Bristol City Museum and Art Gallery, UK/Bridgeman Art Library.

page 47 Madame Doubrere and her Son, 1895 by Louis Valtat (1869–1952). Petit Palais, Geneva, Switzerland/Bridgeman Art Library © ADAGP, Paris and DACS London.

page 50 Mother and Child, c.1893–94 by Pierre Auguste Renoir (1841–1919). National Gallery of Scotland, Edinburgh, Scotland/Bridgeman Art Library.

page 57 A Fair Crop (w/c) by Frederick James McNamara Evans (fl.1886–1930).The Trehayes Collection, Cornwall, UK/Bridgeman Art Library. We have been unable to trace the copyright holder of this painting and would be grateful to receive any information as to their identity.

page 61 Portrait of Mrs George Lewis and her daughter Elizabeth by Sir Lawrence Alma-Tadema (1836–1912). Private Collection/Bridgeman Art Library.

The picture on page 54 is by courtesy of Celia Haddon.

All other pictures are from a private collection.